BRONCO CHARLIE
AND THE
PONY EXPRESS

by Antoine Montero

illustrated by Beth Peck

 HOUGHTON MIFFLIN   BOSTON

A rider appears on the plain. He shimmers in the heat, galloping toward a wooden postal station. By his side is a leather mailbag full of letters and documents that must reach California. As he gets closer and closer to the station, a man steps outside the tiny building. He opens his pocket watch, reads the time, then looks in the rider's direction. He smiles to himself: Right on time, as always!

When the rider comes into the station, he pulls his horse up to a stop. He quickly jumps off and mounts a fresh horse. The station keeper waves to him as he gallops away. He's off again, bringing the mail closer to its final destination and keeping the Pony Express running on time.

From 1860 to 1861 the Pony Express promised to deliver mail from St. Joseph, Missouri to San Francisco, California, in the record time of ten days. Stagecoach trips took months to make the same trip. And sending the mail by ship took even longer, since the ships had to pass all the way around the southernmost tip of South America. But by using fast horses, and plenty of riders to relay the mailbags, the Pony Express was able to make the trip at an amazing pace. More than one hundred riders rode night and day to cover the route of over eighteen hundred miles.

Those eighteen hundred miles ran through some pretty wild country. In the early 1860s, California was bustling and growing quickly. And Missouri was home to growing numbers of settlers, attracted to that state's rich farmland. But in between California and Missouri, settlements were few and far between.

Riding on the Pony Express was dangerous work. The riders faced harsh weather conditions as they rode through the rough lands of the West. They had to pass over the vast High Plains, cross blazing deserts, and climb through frozen mountain passes. Sudden blizzards could sweep through the mountains, dropping several feet of snow. The riders crossed areas that were home to Native Americans who were often hostile to outsiders moving onto their lands, and who might ambush Pony Express riders without warning.

Being a rider took guts, skill, and determination. To find the right people for the job, the owners of the Pony Express ran a newspaper ad. The ad said that riders needed to be: "Young, skinny, wiry fellows not over eighteen. Must be expert riders willing to risk death daily. Orphans preferred."

Charlie Miller fit this description pretty well. He had such a good touch with horses that he had been given the nickname "Bronco Charlie." He wasn't an orphan, but his parents lived far away in New York. Charlie lived on his own in California. And in 1861 he was not yet eighteen—not by a long shot.

The problem was that he was only eleven years old. The
Pony Express wanted young riders who were good with
horses, but not as young as Charlie. Still, as things turned out,
Charlie would get his chance to ride.

The way he told the story years later, Charlie was riding
through the streets of Sacramento, California one day. He
heard hoof beats come up behind him and then watched a
horse ride past. The horse was rider-less, but Charlie saw that
it was carrying a Pony Express bag. Curious, he followed the
horse to the Pony Express station to see what was going
on there.

The men at the station were not happy to see a rider-less horse. They were concerned that something must have happened to the rider on his way into town. But what upset them more was the mail. Without a rider, the Pony Express couldn't possibly meet its schedule. They had to wait for another rider to come in off the trail.

At this point, Charlie piped up and offered to carry the mail for them. On a normal day, they probably would have turned him down, but they were desperate. Speed was everything on the Pony Express. The mail had to keep moving, night and day. Before they could change their minds, Charlie saddled up and rode out of town.

Charlie's goal was to reach Placerville, a town a few dozen miles east of Sacramento. Riding east meant riding up toward the Sierra Nevada mountains. Placerville was nestled there, with the wild mountains looming nearby. It was afternoon when he started, and before long, the sun set and it grew dark.

Charlie rode through the night, all alone on the trail. The land was as rough as could be. "If you wasn't goin' down a trail so steep that your horse would slip forward, why then you was climbin' so hard he'd slip backward!" Charlie recalled. And he was lonely, too. Charlie had spent plenty of nights outside, keeping an eye on cattle or chatting in a camp. But he had never been so alone as he was on that trip, moving down the dark trail, listening to the spooky sounds of the nighttime wilderness. He even missed the company of the cows. "That night was just about the longest I'd ever spent," he once said.

He finally came into Placerville at dawn and rode through its quiet streets to the Pony Express station. The men there were surprised to see him and listened as he told his story. Then the next rider took the mail bag that Charlie brought in and set out on the next leg of the journey: the trail east to Carson City.

Exhausted, Charlie found himself a place to rest and slept for hours. When he woke up, he got some food and returned to the Placerville Pony Express station.

Before too long, Charlie could hear the sounds of a rider coming into town from the east. As the rider drew closer, Charlie could see that something was wrong. The horse was pounding fast down the street. But the rider was wavering unsteadily in the saddle. When horse and rider arrived at the station, Charlie and the others discovered what was wrong. The rider, bleeding from the head, told them he had been attacked on the ride and struck by an arrow!

Charlie didn't have time to listen to the whole story. He took the bag the injured rider had brought in, mounted a new horse, and rode off, heading back to Sacramento.

When Charlie got back to Sacramento, he dropped off the mailbag at the Pony Express office. He was almost reluctant to hand it over, though. Having ridden for the Pony Express twice, he was already falling in love with the work. He wanted more than anything to keep carrying the mail. But now he worried that he had ridden his last ride for the Pony Express.

So Charlie was thrilled the next day when one of the station managers offered him a full-time job! Soon Charlie was reciting the pledge that all the riders made. They promised not to use profane language and not to fight with each other. Then Charlie promised to "conduct myself honestly, be faithful in my duties, and so direct all my acts to win the confidence of my employers."

He carried the mail along the western end of the trail for the next few months. It was hard and dangerous work. Charlie rode through blizzards and heat waves. He was even attacked by Indians and shot with arrows. (When he was an old man, Charlie still loved to show off the scars.) But no matter how tough the job was, Charlie loved it.

Charlie's career with the Pony Express didn't last long. In October of 1861, the first transcontinental telegraph was completed. Messages could now be sent across the country in only minutes. Shortly afterward, the Pony Express shut down. No one needed it anymore, since the messages could move so quickly by telegraph. The last delivery took place on November 30, 1861. Poor Charlie was not even twelve yet and his career as a Pony Express rider was over. But he could say that he was one of only two hundred or so riders ever to serve on the Pony Express. And to Charlie, that meant the world.

For a long time Charlie traveled around the West and worked with horses. Then he worked on Buffalo Bill Cody's Wild West Show. The Wild West Show was like a traveling Western country fair. It was designed to show off the best of the West to people all over the country, and even beyond the United States' borders.

He toured with the Wild West Show for a few years, traveling as far as London, England. Then Charlie left the show. Although he had intended to head back out west, he fell in love with a woman in a small town in New York. He settled there and raised a family and settled into a life far more steady and comfortable than his old one on the frontier.

13

In 1931, seventy years after the Pony Express shut down, Charlie was eighty-one years old and living near New York City. The world had changed greatly from his days as a Pony Express rider. By 1931 airplanes were already crossing the skies and delivering letters by "air mail." And thousands of miles of paved roads let cars drive from city to city all across the country. The days when horses were used for serious travel were long gone and forgotten, Charlie thought.

Because 1931 was an important anniversary for the Pony Express, Charlie wanted to do something special to celebrate. He would ride on horseback from his home in New York to San Francisco in California. His ride would be a tribute to the Pony Express on its seventieth anniversary. So, on July 6th, 1931, he rode his horse Polestar out of New York, carrying a letter from the Mayor of New York to the Mayor of San Francisco.

For the next seven months and twenty-three days, Charlie and Polestar made their way west. They rode along hard-paved roads. They traveled at only a fraction of the speed of the cars that whizzed by them. Charlie often had to search hard to find a stable that could keep Polestar for the night or for a blacksmith who could replace his horseshoes when they wore out or fell off. "There was plenty gasoline stations, and automobile repair places, scattered all along the route, but it was like findin' hen's teeth to find a blacksmith!" Charlie said.

It would have been easy for Charlie to stop riding. After all, who could blame an eighty-one-year-old man for not wanting to complete a ride of over three thousand miles? But he never gave up. After seven months, Charlie and Polestar arrived in San Francisco. Just like in the old days, Charlie delivered his mail. Seventy years and three months after the final Pony Express delivery, Bronco Charlie showed that the spirit of the Pony Express lived on.